A SECOND GOLDEN TREASURY
OF
ANIMAL VERSE

COMPILED BY MARK DANIEL

MACMILLAN CHILDREN'S BOOKS

For Ann

A Second Golden Treasury of Animal Verse

Conceived by Breslich & Foss
This anthology copyright © Breslich & Foss
Designed by Roger Daniels

All rights reserved. No reproduction, copy or transmission of this publication may be made without written permission. No paragraph of this publication may be reproduced, copied or transmitted save with written permission or in accordance with the provisions of the Copyright Act 1956 (as amended). Any person who does any unauthorised act in relation to this publication may be liable to criminal prosecution and civil claims for damages.

First published in Great Britain in 1986 by Pavilion Books Limited
in association with Michael Joseph Limited

Premier Picturemac edition published 1991 by
MACMILLAN CHILDREN'S BOOKS
A division of Macmillan Publishers Limited
London and Basingstoke
Associated companies throughout the world

ISBN 0-333-55194-X

A CIP catalogue record for this book is available from the British Library

Printed in Hong Kong

All colour pictures are courtesy of
Fine Art Photographic Library, London,
except page 61 (Bridgeman Art Library)

Front cover painting by John Hayes (fl. 1897–1902)
Back cover painting Anon (nineteenth century)

Poems by Hilaire Belloc which appear in this
anthology are reprinted by kind permission of
Peters, Fraser & Dunlop Group Ltd

Contents

In the Farmyard
～ 4 ～

Feathered Friends
～ 30 ～

Smallest Creatures
～ 58 ～

The Poets
～ 74 ～
The Painters
～ 76 ～
Index of First Lines
～ 77 ～

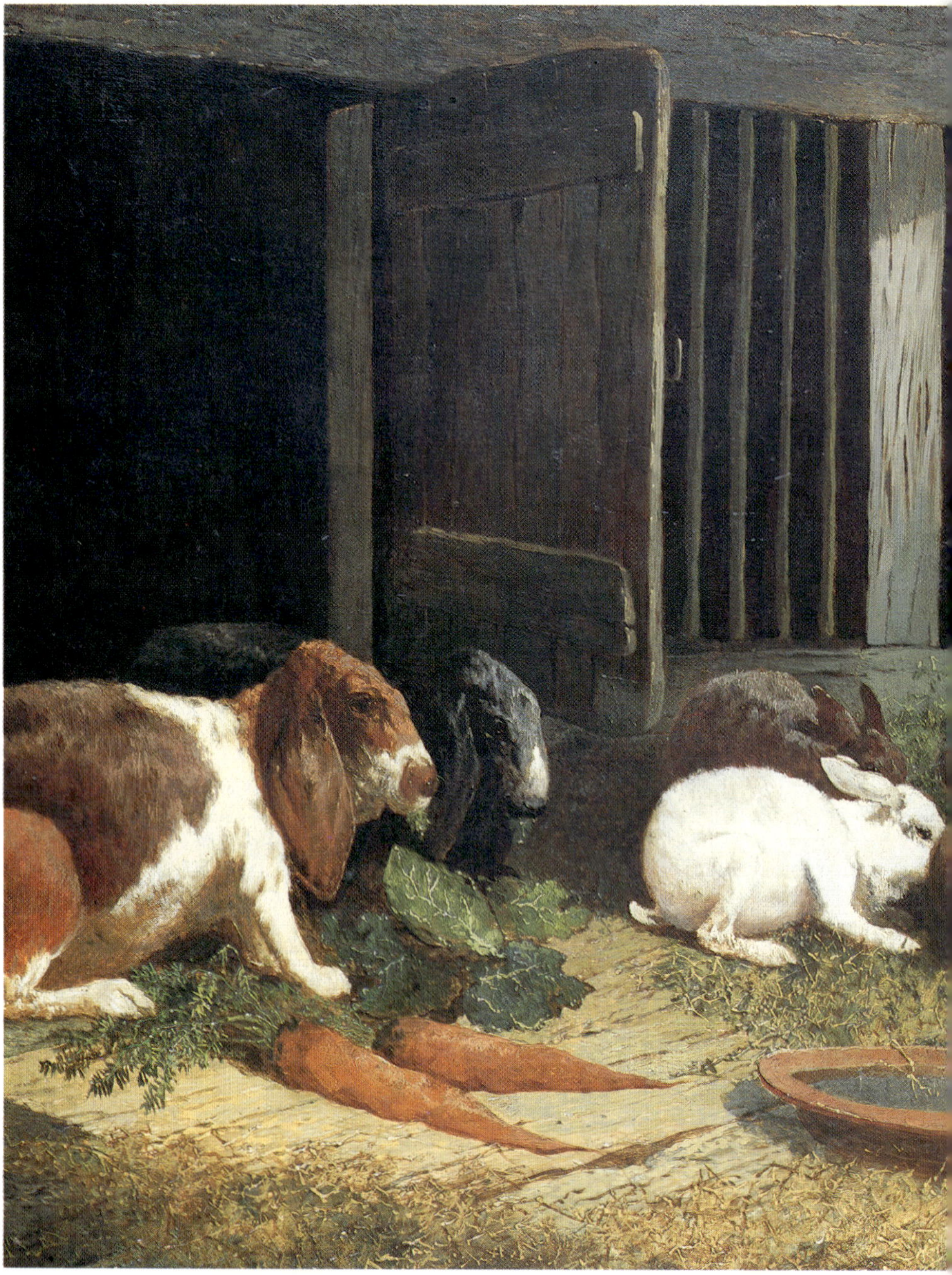

In The Farmyard

POTATO PEEL

Dearly loved children
Is it not a sin
When you peel potatoes,
To throw away the skin?
For the skin feeds pigs
And pigs feed you.
Dearly loved children,
Is this not true?

ANON

THE SHEEP

Lazy sheep, pray tell me why
 In the grassy fields you lie,
Eating grass and daisies white,
From the morning till the night?
Everything can something do,
But what kind of use are you?

Nay, my little master, nay,
Do not serve me so, I pray;
Don't you see the wool that grows
On my back to make you clothes?
Cold, and very cold you'd get,
If I did not give you it.

Sure it seems a pleasant thing
To nip the daisies in the spring,
But many chilly nights I pass
On the cold and dewy grass,
Or pick a scanty dinner where
All the common's brown and bare.

Then the farmer comes at last,
When the merry spring is past,
And cuts my woolly coat away
To warm you in the winter's day;
Little master, this is why
In the grassy fields I lie.

ANN TAYLOR

Goosey, goosey, gander
Where shall I wander?
Upstairs, downstairs,
And in my lady's chamber.
There I met an old man
Who would not say his prayers;
I took him by the left leg
And threw him down the stairs.

ANON

Before the barn door crowing
The cock by hens attended,
His eyes around him throwing,
Stands for a while suspended;
Then one he singles from the crew,
And cheers the happy hen,
With how do you do, and how do you do,
And how do you do again.

JOHN GAY
Fables, 1738

Higgledy, piggledy, my black hen
She lays eggs for gentlemen;
Gentlemen come every day
To see what my black hen doth lay.

ANON

WHAT THE FARMYARD FOWL ARE SAYING

COCK: Lock the dairy door,
Lock the dairy door!

HEN: Chickle, chackle, chee,
I haven't got the key!

ANON

THE GOAT

There was a man, now please take note,
There was a man, who had a goat.
He lov'd that goat, indeed he did,
He lov'd that goat, just like a kid.

One day that goat felt frisk and fine,
Ate three red shirts from off the line.
The man he grabbed him by the back,
And tied him to a railroad track.

But when the train hove into sight,
The goat grew pale and green with fright.
He heaved a sigh, as if in pain,
Coughed up those shirts and flagged the train

ANON

IN THE FARMYARD

THE COW

The friendly cow, all red and white,
 I love with all my heart:
She gives me cream with all her might,
To eat with apple tart.

She wanders lowing here and there,
And yet she cannot stray,
All in the pleasant open air,
The pleasant light of day.

And blown by all the winds that pass
And wet with all the showers,
She walks among the meadow grass
And eats the meadow flowers.

ROBERT LOUIS STEVENSON
A Child's Garden of Verses, 1885

THE LAMB

Little lamb, who made thee?
Dost thou know who made thee,
Gave thee life, and bade thee feed
By the stream and o'er the mead.
Gave thee clothing of delight,
Softest clothing, woolly, bright;
Gave thee such a tender voice,
Making all the vales rejoice?
Little lamb, who made thee?
Dost thou know who made thee?

Little lamb, I'll tell thee;
Little lamb, I'll tell thee:
He is called by thy name,
For He calls Himself a Lamb;
He is meek, and He is mild,
He became a little child.
I a child, and thou a lamb,
We are called by His name.
Little lamb, God bless thee!
Little lamb, God bless thee!

WILLIAM BLAKE
Songs of Innocence, 1789

LAMBS AT PLAY

On the grassy banks
    Lambkins at their pranks;
Woolly sisters, woolly brothers,
Jumping off their feet
While their woolly mothers
Watch by them and bleat.

CHRISTINA ROSSETTI
Sing-Song, 1872

A FRISKY LAMB

A frisky lamb
    And a frisky child
Playing their pranks
In a cowslip meadow:
The sky all blue
And the air all mild
And the fields all sun
And the lanes half shadow.

CHRISTINA ROSSETTI
Sing-Song, 1872

A FARMER'S BOY

They strolled down the lane together,
The sky was studded with stars —
They reached the gate in silence
And he lifted down the bars —
She neither smiled nor thanked him
Because she knew not how;
For he was just a farmer's boy
And she was a jersey cow.

                ANON

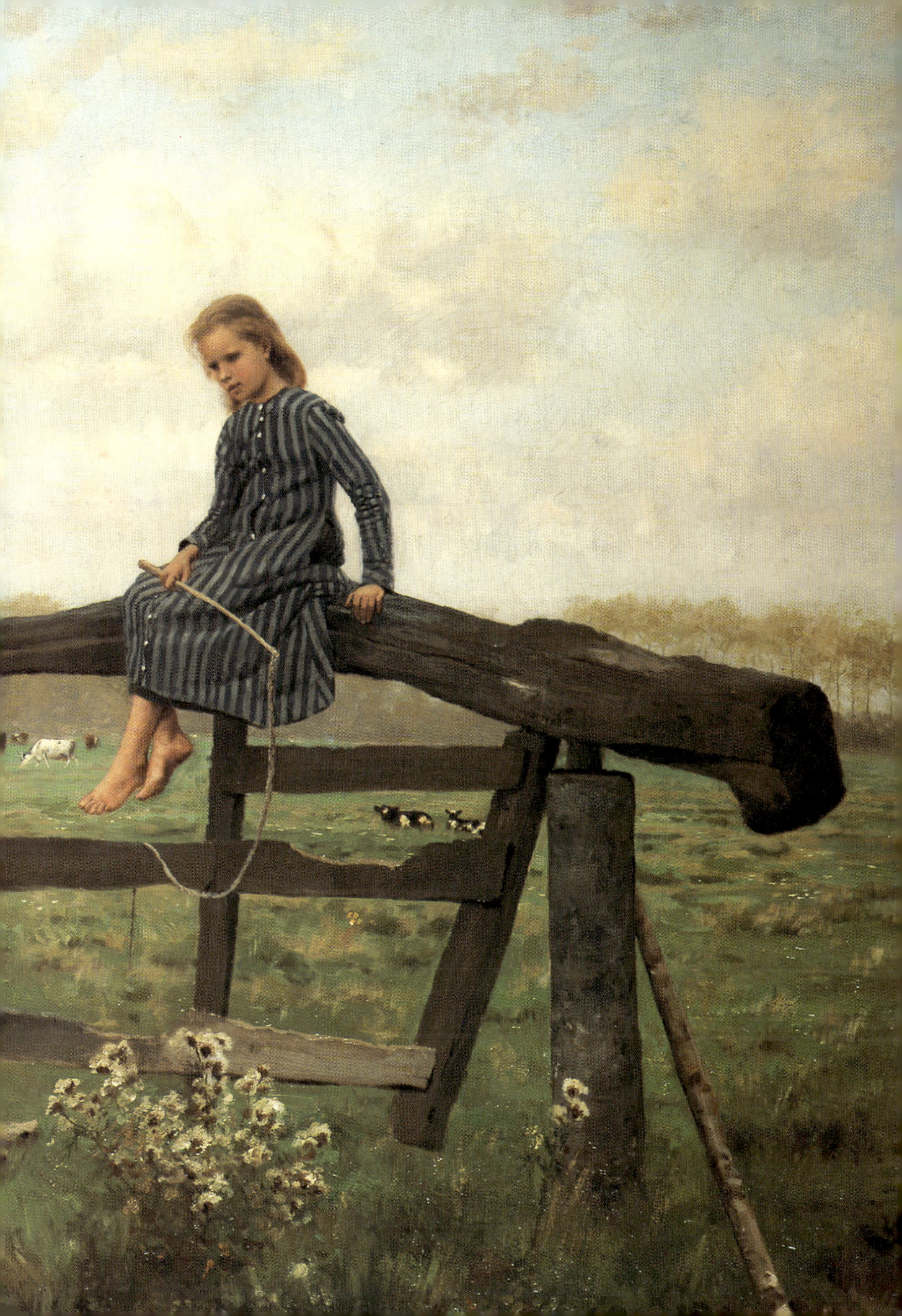

DUCKS' DITTY

All along the backwater,
 Through the rushes tall,
Ducks are a-dabbling,
Up tails all!

Ducks' tails, drakes' tails,
Yellow feet a-quiver,
Yellow bills all out of sight
Busy in the river!

Slushy green undergrowth
Where the roach swim —
Here we keep our larder,
Cool and full and dim!

Every one for what he likes!
We like to be
Heads down, tails up,
Dabbling free!

High in the blue above
Swifts whirl and call —
We are down a-dabbling,
Up tails all!

KENNETH GRAHAME
The Wind In The Willows, 1908

IN THE FARMYARD

THE ROBIN AND THE COWS

The robin sings in the elm;
　The cattle stand beneath,
Sedate and grave with great brown eyes,
And fragrant meadow-breath.

They listen to the flattered bird,
The wise-looking, stupid things!
And they never understand a word
Of all the robin sings.

　　　　　　　WILLIAM DEAN HOWELLS

PIGS

"Do look at those pigs as they lie in the straw,"
Said Dick to his father one day;
"They keep eating longer than I ever saw,
What nasty fat gluttons are they."

"I see they are feasting," his father reply'd,
"They eat a great deal, I allow;
But let us remember, before we deride,
'Tis the nature, my dear, of a sow.

"But when a great boy, such as you, my dear Dick,
Does nothing but eat all the day,
And keeps sucking good things till he makes himself sick,
What a glutton! indeed, we may say.

"When plumcake and sugar for ever he picks,
And sweetmeats, and comfits, and figs;
Pray let him get rid of his own nasty tricks,
And then he may laugh at the pigs."

JANE TAYLOR

BILLY GOAT

There was a young goat named Billy
　Who was more than a little bit silly.
They sent him to school
But he just played the fool
And ate satchels and books willy-nilly.

ANON

Little Bo-peep has lost her sheep,
And can't tell where to find them;
Leave them alone, and they'll come home,
And bring their tails behind them.

Little Bo-peep fell fast asleep,
And dreamt she heard them bleating;
But when she awoke, she found it a joke,
For they were still a-fleeting.

Then up she took her little crook,
Determin'd for to find them;
She found them indeed, but it made her heart bleed,
For they'd left all their tails behind 'em.

ANON

Cushy cow bonny, let down thy milk,
And I will give thee a gown of silk;
A gown of silk and a silver tee,
If thou wilt let down thy milk to me.

ANON

THE COW

Thank you, pretty cow, that made
  Pleasant milk, to soak my bread;
Every day, and every night,
Warm, and fresh, and sweet, and white.

Do not chew the hemlock rank,
Growing on the weedy bank;
But the yellow cowslips eat,
They will make it very sweet.

Where the purple violet grows,
Where the bubbling water flows,
Where the grass is fresh and fine,
Pretty cow, go there and dine.

ANN and JANE TAYLOR

FIVE LITTLE CHICKENS

Said the first little chicken,
   With a queer little squirm,
"Oh, I wish I could find
A fat little worm!"

Said the next little chicken,
With an odd little shrug,
"Oh, I wish I could find
A fat little bug!"

Said the third little chicken,
With a sharp little squeal,
"Oh, I wish I could find
Some nice yellow meal!"

Said the fourth little chicken,
With a small sigh of grief,
"Oh, I wish I could find
A green little leaf!"

Said the fifth little chicken,
With a faint little moan,
"Oh, I wish I could find
A wee gravel stone!"

"Now, see here," said the mother,
From the green garden-patch,
"If you want any breakfast,
You must come here and scratch."

                        ANON

IN THE FARMYARD

THE COW AND THE ASS

Beside a green meadow a stream used to flow,
So clear, you might see the white pebbles below;
To this cooling brook, the warm cattle would stray,
To stand in the shade on a hot summer's day.

A cow quite oppressed by the heat of the sun,
Came here to refresh as she often had done;
And, standing quite still, stooping over the stream
Was musing, perhaps — or perhaps she might
  dream.

But soon a brown ass of respectable look
Came trotting up also to taste of the brook,
And to nibble a few of the daisies and grass.
"How d'ye do?" said the cow. "How d'ye do?" said the
  ass.

"Take a seat!" said the cow, gently waving her hand.
"By no means, dear madam," said he, "while you
  stand!"
Then, stooping to drink, with a very low bow,
"Ma'am, your health!" said the ass.
"Thank you, sir," said the cow.

ANN and JANE TAYLOR

Cackle, cackle, Mother Goose,
Have you any feathers loose?
Truly have I, pretty fellow,
Half enough to fill a pillow.
Here are quills, take one or two,
And down to make a bed for you.

ANON

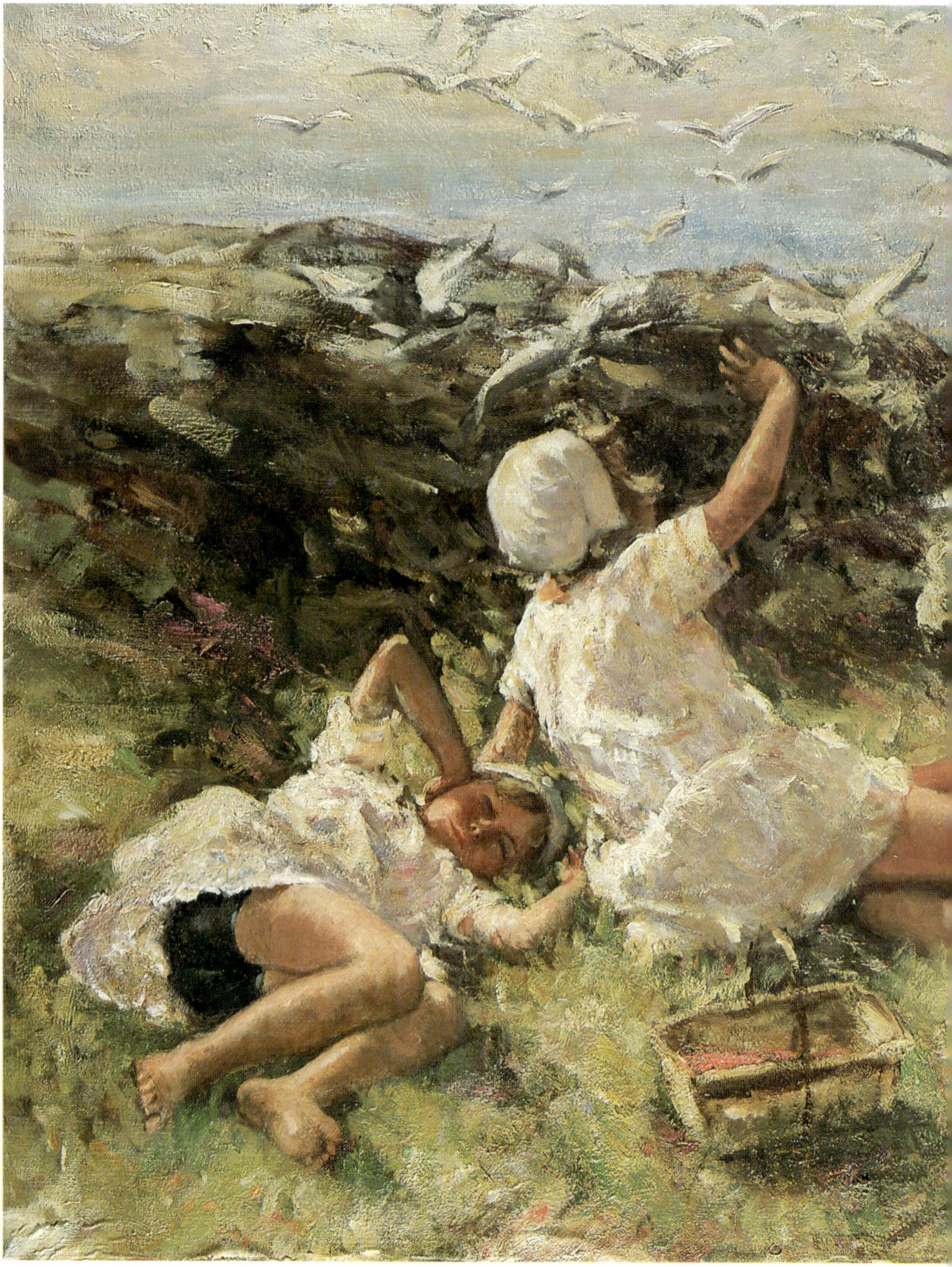

Feathered Friends

THE CROW

Old Crow, upon the tall tree-top
I see you sitting at your ease,
You hang upon the highest bough
And balance in the breeze.

How many miles you've been to-day
Upon your wing so strong and black,
And steered across the dark grey sky
Without a guide or track;

Above the city wrapped in smoke,
Green fields and rivers flowing clear;
Now tell me, as you passed them o'er,
What did you see and hear?

The old crow shakes his sooty wing
And answers hoarsely, "Caw, caw, caw,"
And that is all the crow can tell
Of what he heard and saw.

CECIL FRANCES ALEXANDER
Moral Songs, 1849

CUCKOO

Cuckoo, cuckoo
What do you do?
In April,
I open my bill;
In May,
I sing night and day;
In June,
I change my tune;
In July,
Away I fly;
In August,
Go I must.

ANON

THE OWL

When cats run home and light is come,
   And dew is cold upon the ground,
And the far-off stream is dumb,
   And the whirring sail goes round,
   And the whirring sail goes round;
Alone and warming his five wits,
The white owl in the belfry sits.

When merry milkmaids click the latch,
   And rarely smells the new-mown hay,
And the cock hath sung beneath the thatch
   Twice or thrice his roundelay,
   Twice or thrice his roundelay;
Alone and warming his five wits,
The white owl in the belfry sits.

ALFRED, LORD TENNYSON
Juvenalia, 1830

FEATHERED FRIENDS

Little Trotty Wagtail, he went in the rain,
And tittering tottering sideways, he ne'er got
straight again,
He stooped to get a worm, and looked up to catch
a fly,
And then he flew away ere his feathers they were dry.

Little Trotty Wagtail, he waddled in the mud,
And left his little footmarks, trample where he
would.
He waddled in the water-pudge, and waggle went
his tail,
And chirruped up his wings to dry upon the
garden rail.

Little Trotty Wagtail, you nimble all about,
And in the dimpling water-pudge, you waddle in
and out;
Your home is nigh at hand, and in the warm pig-sty,
So, little Master Wagtail, I'll bid you a good-bye.

JOHN CLARE

THE PARROT

I am the pirate's parrot,
I sail the seven seas
And sleep inside the crow's nest
Don't look for me in trees!

I am the pirate's parrot,
A bird both brave and bold.
I guard the captain's treasure
And count his hoard of gold.

ANON

THE SWALLOW

Fly away, fly away, over the sea,
Sun-loving swallow, for summer is done.
Come again, come again, come back to me,
Bringing the summer and bringing the sun.

CHRISTINA ROSSETTI
Sing-Song, 1872

THE VULTURE

The Vulture eats between his meals
   And that's the reason why
He very, very rarely feels
As well as you and I.

His eye is dull, his head is bald,
His neck is growing thinner.
Oh! what a lesson for us all
To only eat at dinner!

HILAIRE BELLOC
More Beasts for Worse Children, 1897

THE BIRDS

Do you ask what the birds say?
The sparrow, the dove,
The linnet, and thrush say:
I love and I love.

In the Winter they're silent,
The wind is so strong;
What it says I don't know,
But it sings a loud song.

But green leaves and blossoms,
And sunny, warm weather,
And singing and loving,
All come back together.

Then the lark is so brimful
Of gladness and love,
The green fields below him,
The blue sky above,

That he sings and he sings,
And for ever sings he:
I love my love,
And my love loves me.

SAMUEL TAYLOR COLERIDGE

THE SANDPIPER

Across the lonely beach we flit,
  One little sandpiper and I;
And fast I gather, bit by bit,
The scattered driftwood, bleached and dry.
The wild waves reach their hands for it,
The wild wind raves, the tide runs high,
As up and down the beach we flit —
One little sandpiper and I.

Above our heads the sullen clouds
Scud black and swift across the sky;
Like silent ghosts in misty shrouds
Stand out the white lighthouses high.
Almost as far as eye can reach
I see the close-reefed vessels fly,
As fast we flit along the beach —
One little sandpiper and I.

I watch him as he skims along
Uttering his sweet and mournful cry;
He starts not at my fitful song
Or flash of fluttering drapery.
He has no thought of any wrong,
He scans me with a fearless eye;
Staunch friends are we, well-tried and strong,
The little sandpiper and I.

Comrade, where wilt thou be tonight
When the loosed storm breaks furiously?
My driftwood fire will burn so bright!
To what warm shelter canst thou fly?
I do not fear for thee, though wroth
The tempest rushes through the sky:
For are we not God's children both,
Thou, little sandpiper, and I?

CELIA THAXTER
Poems, 1872

BEASTS AND BIRDS

The dog will come when he is called,
The cat will walk away;
The monkey's cheek is very bald,
The goat is fond of play.
The parrot is a prate-apace,
Yet knows not what she says;
The noble horse will win the race,
Or draw you in a chaise.

The pig is not a feeder nice,
The squirrel loves a nut,
The wolf would eat you in a trice,
The buzzard's eyes are shut.
The lark sings high up in the air,
The linnet in the tree;
The swan he has a bosom fair,
And who so proud as he?

ADELAIDE O'KEEFE
Poems For Infant Minds, Vol. II, 1805

FEATHERED FRIENDS

THE SEA-GULL

The waves leap up, the wild wind blows,
And the Gulls together crowd,
And wheel about, and madly scream
To the deep sea roaring loud.
And let the sea roar ever so loud,
And the wind pipe ever so high,
With a wilder joy the bold Sea-gull
Sends forth a wilder cry.

For the Sea-gull, he is a daring bird,
And he loves with the storm to sail;
To ride in the strength of the billowy sea,
And to breast the driving gale!
The little boat, she is tossed about,
Like a sea-weed, to and fro;
The tall ship reels like a drunken man,
As the gusty tempests blow.

But the Sea-gull laughs at the fear of man,
And sails in a wild delight
On the torn-up breast of the night-black sea,
Like a foam cloud, calm and white.
The waves may rage and the winds may roar,
But he fears not wreck nor need;
For he rides the sea, in its stormy strength,
As a strong man rides his steed.

Oh, the white Sea-gull, the bold Sea-gull!
He makes on the shore his nest,
And he tries what the inland fields may be;
But he loveth the sea the best!
And away from land a thousand leagues,
He goes 'mid surging foam;
What matter to him is land or shore,
For the sea is his truest home!

MARY HOWITT
excerpt, Birds and Flowers, 1838

THE EAGLE

He clasps the crag with crooked hands;
Close to the sun in lonely lands,
Ringed with the azure world, he stands.

The wrinkled sea beneath him crawls;
He watches from his mountain walls,
And like a thunderbolt he falls.

ALFRED, LORD TENNYSON
Works, 1907

FEATHERED FRIENDS

THE ROOKS

The rooks are building on the trees;
They build there every spring:
"Caw, caw," is all they say,
For none of them can sing.

They're up before the break of day,
And up till late at night;
For they must labour busily
As long as it is light.

And many a crooked stick they bring,
And many a slender twig,
And many a tuft of moss, until
Their nests are round and big.

"Caw, caw." Oh, what a noise
They make in rainy weather!
Good children always speak by turns,
But rooks all talk together.

JANE EUPHEMIA BROWNE
Aunt Effie's Rhymes For Little Children, 1852

A WARNING

The robin and the redbreast,
The robin and the wren,
If you take them from their nests,
Ye'll ne'er thrive again.

The robin and the redbreast,
The martin and the swallow,
If you touch one of their eggs,
Ill luck is sure to follow.

ANON

BED-TIME

Robin Friend has gone to bed,
Little wing to hide his head.
Mother's bird must slumber, too —
Just as baby robins do.
When the stars begin to rise
Birds and Babies close their eyes.

L. ALMA TADEMA
Realms of Unknown Kings, 1897

The fireside for the cricket,
The wheatstack for the mouse,
When trembling night-winds whistle
And moan all round the house;
The frosty ways like iron,
The branches plumed with snow —
Alas! in winter, dead and dark,
Where can poor Robin go?
Robin, Robin Redbreast,
O Robin dear!
And a crumb of bread for Robin,
His little heart to cheer.

WILLIAM ALLINGHAM
Fifty Modern Poems, 1865

THE BOY AND THE PARROT

"Parrot, if I had your wings
I should do so many things:
I should fly to Uncle Bartle,
Don't you think 'twould make him startle,
If he saw me when I came,
Flapping at the window frame
Exactly like the parrot of fame?"

All this the wise old parrot heard,
The parrot was an ancient bird,
And paused and pondered every word;
First, therefore, he began to cough,
He paused awhile, and coughed again:
"Master John, pray think a little,
What will you do for beds and victual?"

"Oh! parrot, Uncle John can tell —
But we should manage very well;
At night we'd perch upon the trees,
And so fly forward by degrees."

"Does Uncle John," the parrot said,
"Put nonsense in his nephew's head?
I think he might have taught you better,
You might have learnt to write a letter:
That is the thing that I should do
If I had little hands like you."

JOHN HOOKHAM FRERE
excerpt, Fables for Five Years Old, 1830

THE BLOSSOM

Merry, merry sparrow!
Under leaves so green
A happy blossom
Sees you swift as arrow
Seek your cradle narrow
Near my bosom.

Pretty, pretty robin!
Under leaves so green
A happy blossom
Hears you sobbing, sobbing,
Pretty, pretty robin,
Near my bosom.

WILLIAM BLAKE
Songs of Innocence, 1789

I SOMETIMES THINK I'D RATHER CROW

I sometimes think I'd rather crow
And be a rooster than to roost
And be a crow. But I dunno.

A rooster he can roost also,
Which don't seem fair when crows can't crow.
Which may help some. Still I dunno.

Crows should be glad of one thing though;
Nobody thinks of eating crow,
While roosters they are good enough
For anyone unless they're tough.

There're lots of tough old roosters though,
And anyway a crow can't crow,
So mebby roosters stand more show.
It looks that way. But I dunno.

ANON

THE KING-FISHER SONG

King Fisher courted Lady Bird —
Sing Beans, sing Bones, sing Butterflies!
 "Find me my match," he said,
 "With such a noble head —
With such a beard, as white as curd —
 With such expressive eyes!"

"Yet pins have heads," said Lady Bird —
Sing Prunes, sing Prawns, sing Primrose-Hill!
 "And, where you stick them in,
 They stay, and thus a pin
Is very much to be preferred
 To one that's never still!"

"Oysters have beards," said Lady Bird —
Sing Flies, sing Frogs, sing Fiddle-strings!
 "I love them, for I know
 They never chatter so:
They would not say one single word —
 Not if you crowned them Kings!"

"Needles have eyes," said Lady Bird —
Sing Cats, sing Corks, sing Cowslip-tea!
 "And they are sharp — just what
 Your Majesty is *not*:
So get you gone — 'tis too absurd
 To come a-courting *me!*"

LEWIS CARROLL

FEATHERED FRIENDS

The dove says, "Coo,
What shall I do?
I can hardly maintain my two."
"Pooh," says the wren,
"Why, I've got ten
And keep them all like gentlemen!"

ANON

COCK ROBIN

Who killed Cock Robin?
"I," said the Sparrow,
"With my bow and arrow,
I killed Cock Robin."

Who saw him die?
"I," said the Fly,
"With my little eye,
I saw him die."

Who caught his blood?
"I," said the Fish,
"With my little dish,
I caught his blood."

Who'll make his shroud?
"I," said the Beetle,
"With my thread and needle,
I'll make his shroud."

Who'll dig his grave?
"I," said the Owl,
"With my spade and trowel,
I'll dig his grave."

Who'll be the parson?
"I," said the Rook,
"With my little book,
I'll be the parson."

Who'll be the clerk?
"I," said the Lark,
"I'll say Amen in the dark;
I'll be the clerk."

Who'll be chief mourner?
"I," said the Dove,
"I mourn for my love;
I'll be chief mourner."

Who'll bear the torch?
"I," said the Linnet,
"I'll come in a minute,
I'll bear the torch."

Who'll sing his dirge?
"I," said the Thrush,
"As I sing in the bush
I'll sing his dirge."

Who'll bear the pall?
"We," said the Wren,
Both the Cock and the Hen;
"We'll bear the pall."

Who'll carry his coffin?
"I," said the Kite,
"If it be in the night,
I'll carry his coffin."

Who'll toll the bell?
"I," said the Bull,
"Because I can pull,
I'll toll the bell."

All the birds of the air
Fell to sighing and sobbing
When they heard the bell toll
For poor Cock Robin.

ANON

SMALLEST CREATURES

THE FIELDMOUSE

Where the acorn tumbles down,
　Where the ash tree sheds its berry,
With your fur so soft and brown,
With your eye so round and merry,
Scarcely moving the long grass,
Fieldmouse, I can see you pass.

Little thing, in what dark den,
Lie you all the winter sleeping?
Till warm weather comes again,
Then once more I see you peeping
Round about the tall tree roots,
Nibbling at their fallen fruits.

Fieldmouse, fieldmouse, do not go,
Where the farmer stacks his treasure,
Find the nut that falls below,
Eat the acorn at your pleasure,
But you must not steal the grain
He has stacked with so much pain.

Make your hole where mosses spring,
Underneath the tall oak's shadow,
Pretty, quiet, harmless thing,
Play about the sunny meadow.
Keep away from corn and house,
None will harm you, little mouse.

CECIL FRANCES ALEXANDER
Moral Songs, 1849

SMALLEST CREATURES

THE FLY

Little fly,
Thy summer's play
My thoughtless hand
Has brushed away

Am not I
A fly like thee?
Or art not thou
A man like me?

For I dance
And drink and sing
Till some blind hand
Shall brush my wing

If thought is life
And strength and breath
And the want
Of thought is death,

Then am I
A happy fly,
If I live
Or if I die.

WILLIAM BLAKE
Songs of Experience, 1794

Ladybird, ladybird, fly away home;
  Thy house is on fire, thy children all gone —
All but one, and her name is Ann,
And she crept under the pudding-pan.

ANON

SMALLEST CREATURES

THE QUEEN BEE

When I was in the garden,
   I saw a great Queen Bee;
She was the very largest one
That I did ever see.
She wore a shiny helmet
And a lovely velvet gown,
But I was rather sad, because
She didn't wear a crown.

                MARY K. ROBINSON

CATERPILLAR

Brown and furry
Caterpillar in a hurry,
Take your walk
To the shady leaf, or stalk,
Or what not,
Which may be the chosen spot.
No toad spy you,
Hovering bird of prey pass by you;
Spin and die,
To live again a butterfly.

CHRISTINA ROSSETTI
Sing-Song, 1872

Swarms of minnows show their little heads,
   Staying their wavy bodies 'gainst the streams,
To taste the luxury of sunny beams
Tempered with coolness. How they ever wrestle
With their own sweet delight, and ever nestle
Their silver bellies on the pebbly sand.
If you but scantily hold out the hand,
That very instant not one will remain;
But turn your eye, and they are there again.

JOHN KEATS

A NOISELESS PATIENT SPIDER

A noiseless patient spider,
I mark'd where on a little promontory it stood isolated,
Mark'd how to explore the vacant vast surrounding,
It launch'd forth filament, filament, filament, out of itself,
Ever unreeling them, ever tirelessly speeding them.

And you O my soul where you stand,
Surrounded, detached, in measureless oceans of space,
Ceaselessly musing, venturing, throwing, seeking the spheres to connect them,
Till the bridge you will need be form'd, till the ductile anchor hold,
Till the gossamer thread you fling catch somewhere, O my soul.

WALT WHITMAN
Leaves Of Grass, 1855

Great fleas have little fleas upon their backs to bite 'em,
And little fleas have lesser fleas, and so ad infinitum.
And the great fleas themselves in turn have greater
   fleas to go on
While these again have greater still, and greater still,
   and so on.

                  A. DE MORGAN

THE SNAIL

To grass, or leaf, or fruit, or wall,
The Snail sticks close, nor fears to fall,
As if he grew there, house and all
Together.

Within that house secure he hides,
When danger imminent betides
Of storms, or other harm besides,
Of weather.

Give but his horns the slightest touch,
His self-collecting power is such,
He shrinks into his house with much
Displeasure.

Where'er he dwells, he dwells alone,
Except himself has chattels none,
Well satisfied to be his own
Whole treasure.

Thus hermit-like, his life he leads,
Nor partner of his Banquet needs,
And if he meets one, only feeds
The faster.

Who seeks him must be worse than blind
(He and his house are so combined)
If, finding it, he fails to find
Its master.

WILLIAM COWPER
Translations from Vincent Bourne, 1803

UPON A SNAIL

She goes but softly, but she goeth sure,
  She stumbles not, as stronger creatures do;
Her journey's shorter, so she may endure
Better than they which do much further go.

She makes no noise, but stilly seizeth on
The flower or herb appointed for her food;
The which she quietly doth feed upon,
While others range, and glare, but find no good.

And though she doth but very softly go,
However slow her pace be, yet 'tis sure;
And certainly they that do travel so,
The prize which they do aim at, they procure.

JOHN BUNYAN
The Child's John Bunyan, 1929

Today I saw the dragon-fly
Come from the wells where he did lie.

An inner impulse rent the veil
Of his old husk: from head to tail
Came out clear plates of sapphire mail.

He dried his wings: like gauze they grew;
Through crofts and pastures wet with dew
A living flash of light, he flew.

ALFRED, LORD TENNYSON

THE POETS

ALEXANDER, Cecil Frances
(1818–1895) Ireland
Born in Co. Wicklow, Ireland. In 1850 she married the Rev. William Alexander, who was to become Archbishop of Armagh.
Hymns for Little Children (1848) includes not only "All Things Bright and Beautiful" but also "Once in Royal David's City" and "There is a Green Hill Far Away."

ALLINGHAM, William
(1824–1889) Ireland
Born in Ballyshannon in Donegal, Allingham spent most of his life working as a customs officer. His great love for the literature and the peasantry of his native land inspired him to write.

ALMA-TADEMA, Laurence
(1865–1940) UK
Daughter of the pre-Raphaelite painter Sir Lawrence Alma-Tadema and a close friend of the pianist and politician Paderewski, Alma-Tadema died a spinster, as she had prophesied in her famous poem *If No-one Ever Marries Me* (1897).

BELLOC, Joseph Hilaire Pierre
(1870–1953) France
Historian, poet, essayist, novelist, and traveller. Belloc was born near Paris, but was forced to flee with his mother to England by the Franco-Prussian war. An astoundingly prolific author, his more celebrated works include *A Bad Child's Book of Beasts* (1896) and *More Beasts* (1897), from which the verses in this collection are taken; *Danton* (1899); *The Path to Rome* (1902); *Cautionary Tales for Children* (1907); *The French Revolution* (1911); and *The Cruise of "the Nona"* (1925). A devout Catholic and a great friend of G. K. Chesterton, he left an enormous legacy of works characterized by intellectual vigour, euphony, contentiousness, and down-to-earth spirituality.

BLAKE, William
(1757–1827) UK
Poet, painter, and visionary, Blake had no formal education but served an apprenticeship with an engraver. In 1789 he published his *Songs of Innocence*, decorated with his own engravings, then the radical prose work *The Marriage of Heaven and Hell* (1790) and the *Songs of Experience* (1794). A great craftsman and a compulsive worker, Blake wrote verses of deceptive simplicity and sweetness which reveal, however, much righteous anger and fierce idealism.

BROWNE, Jane Euphemia (Aunt Effie)
(1811–1898) UK
Jane Euphemia Browne lived the respectable, restricted life of the well-born, well-to-do Victorian lady, but enjoyed another, secret life in the persona of "Aunt Effie," an enormously popular children's writer and author of *Aunt Effie's Rhymes for Little Children* (1852) and *Aunt Effie's Gift for the Nursery* (1854). She married Stephen Saxby, a Somerset vicar.

BUNYAN, John
(1628–1688) UK
Drafted into Cromwell's parliamentary army, Bunyan devoted much of his life to a study of the Bible. In 1660 he was arrested for preaching without a licence and remained in prison for twelve years, during which he wrote many books; *Grace Abounding to the Chief of Sinners* (1666) and *The Holy City* (1666) being most important. He was released in 1672, but was again arrested. During this period he wrote the first part of his famous *Pilgrim's Progress* (1678). *The Holy War* was published in 1682.

CARROLL, Lewis (Charles Lutwidge Dodgson)
(1832–1898) UK
Lewis Carroll rapidly became famous for his two great works of fantasy and distorted logic, *Alice's Adventures in Wonderland* (1865) and *Through the Looking-glass* (1872), but he was already celebrated in academic circles as a lecturer in mathematics at Oxford. Queen Victoria, expressing her admiration for *Alice*, asked Carroll for a copy of his next book and was dismayed to receive a learned tome about Euclidian geometry.

CLARE, John
(1793–1864) UK
The son of a labourer, rural poet Clare led a picaresque life, his various occupations being listed as "herd-boy, militiaman, vagrant, and unsuccessful farmer." In 1837, after four volumes of his verse had been published, he was declared insane.

COLERIDGE, Samuel Taylor
(1772–1834) UK
Coleridge was a romantic poet, mystic, critic, and scholar. The son of a Devonshire vicar, Coleridge was briefly a soldier, but from 1794

onward concentrated entirely on political reform, journalism, and verse. *Lyrical Ballads* (1798) by Coleridge and his friend Wordsworth contains "Rime of the Ancient Mariner." Other famous poems by Coleridge include "Christabel" (1816) and "Kubla Khan" (1816), though these were in fact far earlier works and by the time of their publication, the poet's health had been broken by opium.

COWPER, William
(1731–1800) UK
Originally trained as a solicitor, Cowper disliked the law and gave it up. He wrote several well-known hymns, some satires, and the well-known "John Gilpin" (1782), "The Task" (1784), and short poems such as "To Mary" (1802). Cowper's style reflects the simplicity of his nature and marks a transition from the formal classicism of the eighteenth century to the freer forms of the nineteenth century.

FRERE, John Hookham
(1769–1846) UK
As a diplomat, Frere served as British envoy to Lisbon (1800–02), Madrid (1802–04), and the Junta (1808–09). He was also one of the founders of two important periodicals of his time. *The Microcosm* (1786–7) and the *Quarterly Review*.

GAY, John
(1685–1732) UK
Balladeer and playwright, Gay was principally famous for two works. *The Beggar's Opera* (1728) and its sequel *Polly* (1729).

GRAHAME, Kenneth
(1859–1922) UK
Grahame's first successful work was *The Golden Age* (1895), a nostalgic collection of studies of childhood, then came *Dream Days* (1898), and the much-loved children's classic *The Wind in the Willows* (1908), in which the perennial favourites Toad, Ratty, Mole, and Badger first saw the light of day.

HOWELLS, William Dean
(1837–1920) USA
American novelist and critic, Howells was the editor of the *Atlantic Monthly* (1872) and associate editor of *Harper's Magazine* (1886–91). He was a prolific writer of literary articles and of romances.

HOWITT, Mary (née Botham)
(1799–1888) UK
Wife of author William Howitt and mother of twelve children, Mary Howitt, a Quaker, collaborated with her husband and published more than a hundred books in her own right. Among other claims to fame, she was the first English translator of Hans Christian Andersen.

KEATS, John
(1795–1821) UK
The son of a livery stable-keeper in London, Keats was apprenticed to an apothecary but turned instead to surgery before his enthusiasm for literature got the better of him. His great sonnet "On First Looking into Chapman's Homer" was published by Leigh Hunt in the *Examiner* in 1816, to be followed by "The Poems" of 1817. Then came "Endymion" (1818) and a host of great poems, including "The Eve of St. Agnes," "La Belle Dame Sans Merci," and the magnificent autumn odes, "On a Grecian Urn," "To A Nightingale," "To Autumn," and "On Melancholy." Keats died of tuberculosis in 1821.

DE MORGAN, Mary Augusta
(1850–1907) UK
Sister of the pre-Raphaelite William de Morgan, Mary Augusta de Morgan wrote several collections of fairy stories, such as *On a Pincushion and other Fairy Tales* (1877) and *The Windfairies and other Tales* (1900).

O'KEEFE, Adelaide
(1776–1855) UK
Like the Taylors, Adelaide O'Keefe contributed to the collection *Original Poems for Infant Minds*. Although a collection of her own poems, *Original Poems: Calculated to Improve the Mind of Youth*, was also published, O'Keefe spent most of her life caring for her blind father.

ROSSETTI, Christina Georgina
(1830–1894) UK
Sister of the poet and painter Dante Gabriel Rossetti, Christina led a sad life and failed to fulfil her early exceptional promise. She twice rejected suitors because of her high Anglican religious principles, and her verses are devout and full of the sadness of "what might have been." Her first collection, *Goblin Market* (1862), is her finest, but *Sing-Song* (1872) is full of charming, simple verses for children. She was always frail and, at the time of *Sing-Song*'s composition, was very close to death from Grave's disease. Thereafter she taught with her mother and wrote "morally improving" verse.

THE POETS

STEVENSON, Robert Louis
(1850–1894) UK
Stevenson was a master stylist and supremely imaginative writer who contrived to lead a hero's life despite often crippling illness. All his life he suffered from chronic bronchial problems and acute nervous excitability. Stevenson nonetheless travelled extensively, wrote many fine essays and novels, and in *A Child's Garden of Verses* (1885) applied his highly developed gifts of imagination and sympathy to the emotions and enthusiasms of childhood. In so doing he can be said to have invented a whole new genre of verse. In 1888 he travelled in the South Seas and at last settled with his family in Samoa, where the natives called him "Tusitala" (the tale-teller). He died there of a brain haemorrhage. His novels include *Treasure Island* (1883), *Kidnapped* (1886), *Catriona* (1893), and for older readers the eerie *Strange Case of Dr Jekyll and Mr Hyde* (1886).

TAYLOR, Jane and Ann
(1783–1824) UK
With her sister Ann, Jane Taylor was the best known children's poet of her time. They lived together at their family home in Colchester, Essex.

TENNYSON, Alfred Lord
(1809–1892) UK
Although the most honoured poet of the Victorian era, Tennyson liked to live "far from the madding crowd" in Hampshire or on the Isle of Wight. He was very prolific and although he never wrote specifically for children, many of his works have become firm favourites with young people because of their grand romantic subject matter or because they are ideal for reciting.

THAXTER, Celia (née Laighton)
(1835–1894) USA
Born in Portsmouth, New Hampshire, Thaxter's father was an ambitious politician. When he failed to be elected state governor, he decided on a whim to be a lighthouse-keeper. Celia, therefore, who had been used to a rich world with lots of company, now found herself growing up with her two brothers and a lot of seabirds on the Isle of Shoals, ten miles from the mainland. She married and moved back to the mainland but in 1866 returned to the solitude of her beloved island.

WHITMAN, Walt
(1819–1892) USA
Initially a printer and only an occasional writer, Whitman seemed set for a successful career as an editor, but his political integrity hindered him and he found himself earning a living as a carpenter and builder until he published the startlingly original *Leaves of Grass* in 1855. At first ill-received it slowly grew in popularity until his then employer – the government – became aware of their lowly clerk's part-time job and dismissed him on the grounds of the book's "immorality." This caused a furor which at once sold many copies of the book and helped Whitman earn the enormous reputation he enjoys today.

THE PAINTERS

page	
Title	Robert Gemmel Hutchinson (1855–1936)
4	John Frederick Herring (1795–1865)
8	William Weeks (fl. 1864–1904)
9	Cornelius Van Leemputten (1841–1902)
12	Julian Dupré (1851–1910)
16	Emile Claus (1849–1924)
19	Edward Neale (fl. 1858–1881)
22	Johan Mari Ten Kate (1831–1910)
23	F. Blacklock (fl. 1872–1922)
27	Julian Dupré (1851–1910)
30	Robert Gemmel Hutchinson (1855–1936)
35	Lilian Medland (nineteenth century)
38	Archibald Thorburn (1860–1935)
43	A. Bailey (nineteenth century)
46	John Cyril Harrison (fl. 1882–1891)
50	Henry Carter (fl. 1860–1894)
55	Anon (nineteenth century)
58	Andreas Theodor Mattenheimer (1787–1856)
61	George Thomas Rope (1846–1929)
64	Edward Julius Detmold (1883–1957)
66	Eloise Harriet Stannard (fl. 1852–1893)
67	Percy Tarrant (fl. 1881–1930)
71	Johan Laurentz Jensen (1800–1856)
72	William Hutton (nineteenth century)
78	John Hayes (fl. 1897–1902)

INDEX OF FIRST LINES

A frisky lamb	15	I am the pirate's parrot	37	The dog will come when he is called	42
A noiseless patient spider	68	I sometimes think I'd rather crow	53	The dove says "Coo"	55
Across the lonely beach we flit	40	King Fisher courted Lady Bird –	54	The fireside for the cricket	50
All along the backwater	18			The friendly cow, all red and white	13
Before the barn door crowing	9	Ladybird, ladybird, fly away home	63	The robin and the redbreast	49
Beside a green meadow a stream used to flow	28	Lazy sheep, pray tell me why	7	The robin sings in the elm	20
Brown and furry	66	Little Bo-peep has lost her sheep	23	The rooks are building on the trees	48
Cackle, cackle, Mother Goose	29	Little fly	62	The Vulture eats between his meals	38
Cock: Lock the dairy door	10	Little lamb, who made thee?	14	The waves leap up	44
Cuckoo, cuckoo	33	Little Trotty Wagtail	36	There was a man, now please take note	11
Cushy cow bonny, let down thy milk	24	Lock the dairy door	10	There was young goat named Billy	22
		Merry, merry sparrow!	52	They strolled down the lane together	16
Dearly loved children	6	Old crow upon the tall tree-top	32	Today I saw the dragon-fly	72
Do look at those pigs	21	On the grassy banks	15	To grass, or leaf, or fruit or wall	70
Do you ask what the birds say?	39	Parrot, if I had your wings	51	When cats run home	34
Fly away, fly away, over the sea	37	Robin Friend has gone to bed	49	When I was in the garden	65
Great fleas have little fleas	69	Said the first little chicken	26	Where the acorn tumbles down	60
Goosey, goosey, gander	8	She goes but softly	71	Who killed Cock Robin?	56
He clasps the crag with crooked hands	46	Swarms of minnows show their little heads	67		
Higgledy, piggledy, my black hen	10	Thank you, pretty cow	25		

Also available: A First Golden Treasury of Animal Verse

Other Premier Picturemacs you will enjoy

The Christmas Handbook   Malcolm Bird/Alan Dart
Jack The Treacle Eater   Charles Causley/Charles Keeping
A First Golden Treasury of Children's Verse   Mark Daniel
A Second Golden Treasury of Children's Verse   Mark Daniel
A First Treasury of Fairy Tales   Michael Foss
A Second Treasury of Fairy Tales   Michael Foss
Black Beauty   Anna Sewell/Robin McKinley/Susan Jeffers
The Magic Ointment   Eric Quayle/Michael Foreman
The Enchanter's Spell   Gennady Spirin
The Enchanted World Part One   Amabel Williams-Ellis/Moira Kemp
The Enchanted World Part Two   Amabel Williams-Ellis/Moira Kemp

For a complete list of Picturemac and Premier Picturemac titles write to:

Macmillan Children's Books, 18–21 Cavaye Place,
London SW10 9PG